Mindset Makeover

# *The Resilient Leader*

## Study Guide

Cynthia Howard PhD, LSSBB

Copyright Notice

Copyright 2023 ©, Cynthia Howard PhD, LSSBB   All Rights Reserved.

ISBN: 978-0-692-06377-4

No part of this work may be reproduced or transmitted in any form by any means, electronic or mechanical, including photocopying, without written permission by the author.

Worksmartclubnetwork.com

# CONTENTS

Overview .................................................................................................... 6
   The Value of Reflection ........................................................................ 7
   Coachable Mindset ............................................................................... 8
Why Resilience? ...................................................................................... 9
   Pressure vs Performance Chart ......................................................... 13
   Creating Your Personal Dashboard ................................................... 16
      Study Questions ............................................................................. 17
Common Energy Drains ........................................................................ 19
      Study Questions ............................................................................. 20
   Perfectionism ...................................................................................... 23
      Study Questions ............................................................................. 23
   The Value of Your Time ..................................................................... 25
      Study Questions ............................................................................. 25
Bias (Mindset Distortions) ..................................................................... 30
      Study Questions (Bias) .................................................................. 30
Habits ..................................................................................................... 32
      Study Questions ............................................................................. 32
   Daily Review ....................................................................................... 35
   Habit Tracker ...................................................................................... 35
Optimism (Untapped Resource) ............................................................ 36
      Study Questions ............................................................................. 36
   Fatal Emotions ................................................................................... 37
      Study Questions ............................................................................. 38
Resilient Thinking .................................................................................. 42
   Activate Your Resilient Thinking ....................................................... 42
   Boost Your Resilient Thinking ........................................................... 43
      Study Questions ............................................................................. 44

Action Plan .................................................................................................................... 46
    Goal Worksheet ........................................................................................................ 47
Notes ............................................................................................................................ 48
Benefits of Coaching ................................................................................................. 49
    Coaching Really Works (Research Findings) ............................................... 50
  Value Contributions (Why Work Smart Coaches are the Best Coach for You): ..................... 51
About Work Smart Club ........................................................................................... 52
About Dr. Howard ..................................................................................................... 53

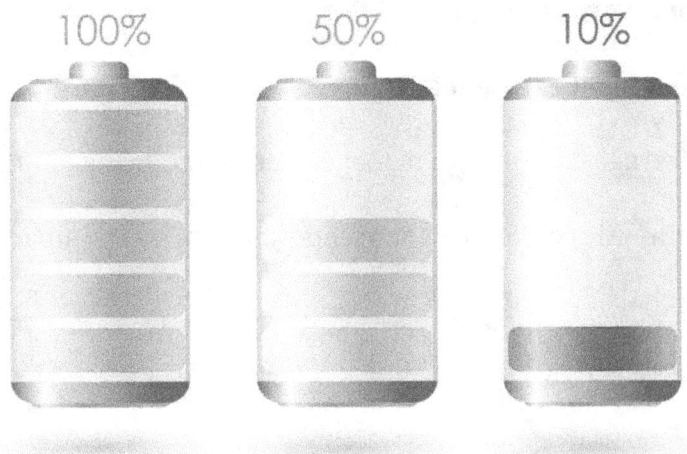

*From idea to impact*

*... your capacity as a leader* drives your success.

# OVERVIEW

Resilience is a set of skills that is overlooked for its power to transform leadership from mediocre to effective and consistent.

**To lead others, you must first understand you.**

Through this online training and coaching you will strengthen your resilience and learn new skills to *flourish* in a demanding environment.

> **As a result of this program, you will:**
>
> 1. Increase your agility and effectiveness.
>
> 2. Learn to leverage emotions to manage change and bring out the best in people.
>
> 3. Develop authentic confidence for greater influence and impact.

**The online course follows this study guide.**

Check your emails for your login information and other important reminders and tips to make this program a success.

The Work Smart Club is dedicated to your growth and success as a leader and want you to experience more satisfaction in your life. Explore the online membership site, take advantage of the resources available.

Questions? Post them in the Network.

Interested in 1:1 coaching email contact@worksmartclubnetwork.com and put 1:1 Coaching in the subject line.

# The Value of Reflection

Self-awareness is a critical "skill" for effective leaders. Your study guide offers many opportunities to reflect and learn more about you. This "getting to know you" process, while uncomfortable, at times, is designed to unleash your hidden potential.

Embrace the chance to learn more about you. Develop a new habit of reflection and you will learn, grow, and perform better.

**Benefit of reflection:**

- ❖ It helps you understand the experience at a deeper level, increasing your insights.

- ❖ As you learn more about you, you become more authentic.

- ❖ Reflection helps you connect the dots between what you do and why you are doing it. It is an opportunity to evaluate your values and your alignment of those values.

- ❖ Reflection develops higher-level thinking and problem-solving ability, something that will set you apart from other leaders.

- ❖ This helps you move forward even during the toughest times by learning from your experiences.

Reflection helps you internalize the new behaviors more quickly. It is not enough to just think about the answers, it is necessary to write them out.

**Writing engages more of your brain. People who have written out their goals and have an accountability partner are 76% more likely to achieve success.**

We are your accountability partner, and this program is designed to help you succeed.

Make reflection a new habit for resilient, engaged, and authentic leadership.

 Download the Element of Reflection steps in the online program. Watch the short video outlining each step.

## Coachable Mindset

Being coachable is a valuable trait. It is

**the willingness to learn X the willingness to act.**

Being willing to learn means you give up control and embrace what you do not know. It is the ability to receive feedback and learn. This is the first part of the equation. You must also be willing to act. What are you going to do about what you learned?

Emotional intelligence is one of the areas many leaders ignore. As an example, an executive may hear something about empathy and say, "Yeah, yeah, I know I have to listen more..." and then proceed to tune out everything else, completely missing the deeper points around how to be present to people. Unfortunately, leaders who fail to relate to their staff and people around them impact the bottom line!

Keep an open mind as you go through this program.

Being coachable means you are open, curious, asking questions and trying out new behaviors. You have turned on your self-awareness and begin to recognize how your thoughts and actions impact others and your desired outcome.

The opposite is to be resistant to anything new. This shows up with apathy, indifference, and going through the motions at work.

Coachability is one of the most desired traits in your followers – why not role model this for them!

 The online module has a checklist to download that will build your awareness around those triggers that block your coachability.

# WHY RESILIENCE?

We are living and working in a world with an 8 second attention span. Technology has changed how we communicate and learn. Most people have not associated their increase in urgency and loss of peace with the increased use of technology.

Information overload is real.

> 2.7 billon Google searches in <u>2006</u> – NOW 31 billon searches <u>every month</u>. More information will be generated this year than in the previous 5,000 years.

The tools in this coaching series will help you make the 3 mindset shifts that will power up your leadership.

> *What you feel, how you think and what you do are subject to how you perceive what is happening around you.*

**A resilient mindset increases your capacity.**

Capacity is how much of something you have. Just like your smart phone, when you have a fully charged battery, you can use all the apps and maximize the use of your phone.

**What is it like for you when you are resilient? What do you notice?**

**What could you accomplish with greater capacity? Identify one thing you want to achieve but fall short due to lack of energy. Write out the details.**

**In what areas would you like your leadership to improve?**

- ☐ Communication
- ☐ Organization
- ☐ Decision Making
- ☐ Dealing with change
- ☐ Team Building
- ☐ Managing my stress
- ☐ Presenting my ideas
- ☐
- ☐
- ☐
- ☐

Do you have a plan to develop these areas: If yes, write it out:

# Pressure vs Performance Chart

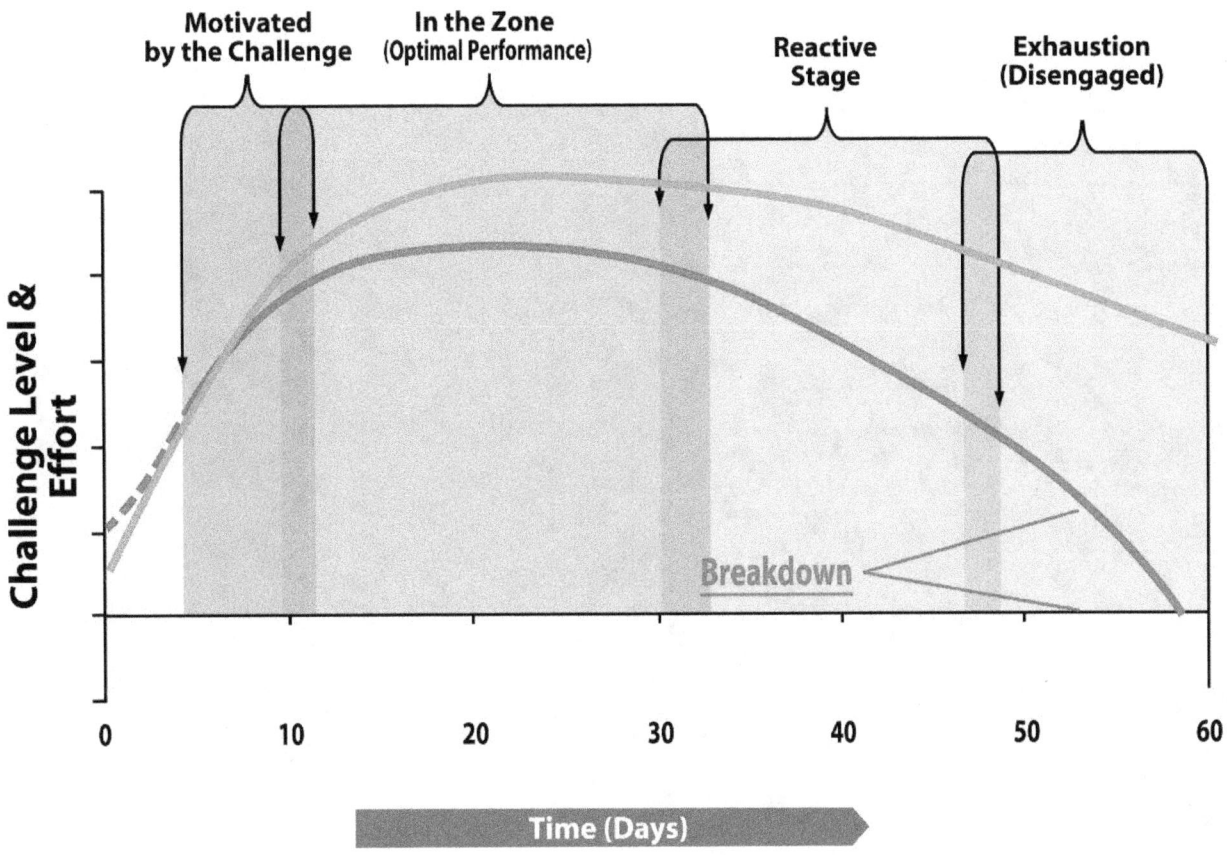

Where are you now on this map?

Think about when you were working in the "Maximum Efficiency Zone," what helped you stay there?

What will you do differently to get back to the "Maximum Efficiency Zone?"

## Creating Your Personal Dashboard

Your personal dashboard is a visual tool to help you quickly see the impact of stress and pressure. Use the chart below to get started. Visit the online portal to download the Personal Dashboard handout.

In the first column, make a list of descriptors when you are at your peak (full capacity). In the second column list those things that drain your energy (warning lights). In the third column, list strategies that help you stay energized, like drinking more water, exercise, deliberate breathing, mindful attention, etc.

**Your capacity drives your performance** and your ability to enjoy your life. Seeing this chart can help you understand how you operate when you aren't feeling your best and how that compares to your full potential. When one of these warning lights comes up, you'll be better prepared to react appropriately and correct your course.

| Personal Indicators | Warning Lights | Strategies |
| --- | --- | --- |
|  |  |  |

## STUDY QUESTIONS

**1.** What are some of your warning lights that let you know you aren't performing to your full capacity?

**2.** How do the following affect your performance: not enough sleep, hunger, a fight with your significant other, bad traffic, an unexpected bill in the mail?

3. Do you pay attention to your warning lights, or do you prefer to keep them "out of sight, out of mind"? Do you consider yourself self-aware?

4. What pressure are you facing right now, at home or at work? What are some techniques you can use to handle pressure and still perform at a high level?

5. How do your emotions at work carry over to your emotions at home, and vice versa?

# COMMON ENERGY DRAINS

Distractions, delays, misunderstanding fill the typical workday making it difficult to make progress. This is the vicious cycle of distraction. Making progress is a major motivator for people and the chronic distraction dulls the momentum.

**Does this sound like your typical day at work?**

- » 2-3 hours, daily, on emails alone.
- » Every three minutes there is an interruption.
- » 50% of what is done is a do-over.
- » 70% of errors are due to a communication breakdown.
- » Roughly $500 billion is lost because of workplace stress.
- » 70% of workers are on autopilot.

Did you know a 15 second distraction costs 20 minutes in concentration?

Work has become a major stressor for people. Communication breakdowns, conflict, initiative overload, bad bosses, complexity, and daily hassles interfere with getting the job done.

Did you know…

*You can get beyond the distractions, stress, and internal emotional distress that distorts your ability to communicate with resilient thinking and focus?*

The brain has a mental default mode and fills in words or solutions—even if they are not there—to bridge a gap. Your mental default mode goes into gear when you are under stress. The longer you look at a problem, in the same way, the more likely you will get stuck in destructive thought loops.

Is your mental default to obsess about problems?

This is limiting!

## STUDY QUESTIONS

1. Think about your most recent workday. Make a list of the distractions you faced from the time you woke up to the time you fell asleep. How could you have reacted differently to these distractions to exhibit resilience?

2. In general, do you anticipate change or react to change? Give an example of how you handled a recent change.

3. Do you consider yourself flexible or rigid? Give an example of why you chose that description.

**4.** Do you feel like you have authentic confidence, or do you feel like you're always in a "fake it till you make it" situation?

**5.** When was the last time you avoided a challenge because you didn't think you could handle it? Write out an example.

**6.** How much of your time and resources do you devote to developing your mindset? How could you improve this and make it a priority?

# Perfectionism

The struggle with **perfectionism** is directly related to self-doubt and a lack of boundaries. It means never knowing when enough is enough, never knowing when you've reached your full capacity. If you're always striving to "be the best you can be," you need to make sure you recognize what your best looks like.

It starts with healthy self-awareness and confidence. You must face your fear of criticism, fear of inadequacy, fear of failure, and fear of making critical decisions. All these fears hold you back from *actually* being your best and overcoming them will require you to set aside your perfectionism and replace it with a more well-rounded mindset.

## STUDY QUESTIONS

1. Do you consider yourself a perfectionist? Why or why not?

2. Describe the last time you felt like you truly "did your best."

3. How do you react when you receive criticism (constructive or otherwise)?

4. Has the fear of failure or "not being good enough" held you back from any of your goals? Describe when and how.

# The Value of Your Time

If **time** is your most valuable resource, how much of it are you willing to sacrifice for trivial reasons? Your workday might be full of distractions that don't contribute to your "big picture," but it feels like you have to wade through all the mess before getting to what's really important. You might spend most of your day answering repeated questions, redoing tasks that weren't done properly the first time, or bridging communication gaps between people who should be able to communicate directly.

If your workday leaves you drained and overwhelmed instead of energized and motivated, it might be time to look at everything that steals your time throughout the day and decide which things are constructive and which are destructive. Build new strategies to manage interruptions, set boundaries between your personal life and work, fight procrastination, and set meaningful and achievable goals. When you prioritize correctly, your time will go to the most important things first—instead of the other way around.

## STUDY QUESTIONS

1. What do you consider the most important part of your job description? How much time do you spend focused on those tasks?

2. Calculate the value of your time. Start with your base salary. Add in the value of your benefits, paid leave, healthcare, and any other perks you receive.

   Total Salary + Benefit Package: _____

   How many hours are you expected to spend at your job? _____
   (This may be different from the number of hours you spend at your job.)

   Divide your salary and benefit package by the number of hours and you have a basic valuation of your time.

3. How much time in a typical workday do you spend handling things that don't relate to your own job? Write out examples of activities that you are engaged in, that takeaway from your most important work.

**4.** Complete the Priority Matrix. In which areas do you think you're losing the most energy in a typical day?

| Urgent | Important |
|---|---|
| | |

| Not Urgent | Not Important |
|---|---|
| | |

5. Which of these common stressors at work do you feel best applies to you: not enough time, too much to do and lack of priorities, the status quo, or office politics and drama?

6. Do you experience drama at work? Does the drama usually originate from you or other people?

**7.** Do you struggle with setting boundaries between work and home? What steps can you take to draw a stronger boundary?

# BIAS (MINDSET DISTORTIONS)

**Bias** in our thinking (also known as cognitive distortions) are inherent in everyone and impact decision-making in many ways. When you make a decision, you bring all of your biases to the table along with your logic and reasoning skills. Biases are subconscious and hard to identify in yourself unless you're paying close attention. Some examples include blind spot bias, confirmation bias, the anchoring effect, optimism bias, availability bias, and estimation bias.

## STUDY QUESTIONS (BIAS)

1. How often do you make conscious, impartial decisions? Are you more inclined to "go with your gut" and listen to your instincts instead?

2. Can you think of a time when your personal bias impacted a decision you made? How do you feel when you reflect on your decision?

**3.** As you review the list of common biases, which ones stand out to you that you recognize in yourself? In your peers?

**4.** What experiences in your life do you think have contributed to the biases you have now?

# HABITS

Every day, you carry out dozens of **habits** without even thinking about it. You may have developed them consciously, like a new diet, or subconsciously, like taking a certain route to work every morning to avoid traffic. Some habits are important ways to take care of yourself (brushing your teeth, washing your face, calling a friend every week to check in), but other habits can be detrimental to your health (binging on cookies when you're stressed, biting your nails, staying up late). If you are always distracted, you'll develop more and more habits as time goes on because your mind is desperate to save energy.

Not only that, but some habits can lay the foundation for other habits, creating a snowball effect. Increasing your awareness of all your habits—good and bad—can help you stay focused and intentional throughout your day. Mindfulness is the best way to identify your habits and stop the habits that are hurting you.

## STUDY QUESTIONS

1. Describe your daily routine in detail. What parts of your routine do you consider long-lasting habits?

2. Do you think it would be difficult to introduce a new habit into your routine? Why or why not?

3. Which of your habits are keeping you from improving yourself and moving forward?

4. How can you replace your bad habits with new, better habits?

5. Make a brief action plan for how you can follow through with changing your habits. What steps will you take? Who will keep you accountable? How will you handle setbacks? How will you reward yourself when you achieve your goal?

| Habits to Change | Desired Habit | Potential Barriers |
|---|---|---|
|  |  |  |

ACTION PLAN:

| | | |
|---|---|---|
|  |  |  |

ACTION PLAN:

| | | |
|---|---|---|
|  |  |  |

ACTION PLAN:

| | | |
|---|---|---|
|  |  |  |

ACTION PLAN:

| | | |
|---|---|---|
|  |  |  |

ACTION PLAN:

## Daily Review

Check out the module online with instructions on the Daily Review. This is a power habit and we highly recommend it.

## Habit Tracker

The Habit Tracker is a daily checklist you can use to build your new power habits. You can download this online.

# OPTIMISM (UNTAPPED RESOURCE)

Optimism is a way of looking at the circumstances around you and it is based on a feeling of confidence that the problems one is facing are not bigger than they are. Optimism enables you to balance the pressure of the challenge with your ability to get through it.

## STUDY QUESTIONS

1. Do you consider yourself an optimist? Why?

2. Pessimists consider things as permanent, "Nothing will ever changes," pervasive, "Everything is all wrong," personal, "I must attract bad things." Think about a time when you feel into that thinking, what was going on?

## Fatal Emotions

Most people go through the day reacting to different situations and challenges that arise, never stopping to think about and question why they feel the way they feel. But one of the best ways to understand and control your thoughts and actions is to tame your emotions, and that starts by identifying each emotion as it arises.

Consider the following emotions: **anger**, **happiness**, **anxiety**, **fear**, and **sadness**. Each of these emotions tells you something important when you feel it and ignoring them can lead to serious consequences. Pushing down an emotion can cause it to surge until you can't control it anymore. Fatal emotions like **discouragement** and **denial** can even have long-lasting effects like resistance to change and a lack of self-confidence. When you name and face your emotions head-on, you can handle them appropriately and build self-awareness, focus, and optimism.

We have all received some type of disappointing news. Your promotion did not come through, the raise wasn't what you expected, you lost the bid for the job, you did not get accepted into your program—the list can go on.

Disappointment is part of living life. When you do not manage those disappointments and you become discouraged, that can be fatal. Discouragement that goes unchecked destroys self-image, confidence, and expectations for the future.

### Discouragement

The dictionary definition of discouragement is "the act of making something less likely to happen." When discouragement is left unchecked, it can grow into a mood, eroding motivation, and momentum.

The erosion can be subtle. The discouragement shifts to a feeling that "things will never work out." You may try harder only to experience more disappointment, or you may give up altogether. Either way, discouragement kills drive.

When you can identify your feelings, you will be able to take the right action to shift them.

### Go from Discouraged to Determined

1. **Name it:** Whenever you feel disappointed, identify it and act.

2. **Reframe it**: Identify three things that are going well for you.

3. **Claim it**: Engage the optimist in you and recognize that it is not permanent, and things will change. Denial is what makes this emotion fatal, capable of destroying your mojo.

4. **Talk about it:** (Or write in your journal.) Find a safe person who will simply listen. At this point, talking it out helps release the heavy emotion. You can find solutions later.

5. **Help someone else**: The tendency with discouragement is to narrow your focus and think only of your problems. Get out of yourself and reach out to someone in need.

## STUDY QUESTIONS

1. Which emotions do you find harder to handle than others? Are there certain emotions that can completely derail you when they arise?

2. When you feel discouraged, what do you need to hear from yourself and other people around you to handle it appropriately?

**3.** When was the last time you experienced denial? Do you feel like you overcame it, or do you still get stuck?

|  |
|--|
|  |

**4.** How do you think your personal fears contribute to your emotions of anger, anxiety, or fear?

|  |
|--|
|  |

**5.** Review the feeling chart on the next page. Write down those emotions you experience often. In the second column, write down those you do not experience very often.

*Do you need to expand your emotional vocabulary?*

Fill in those emotions below.

| Emotions Experienced Often | Emotions Not Experienced |
|---|---|
|  |  |

*Grab your Emotions card that came in your packet. A copy of it is on the next page.*

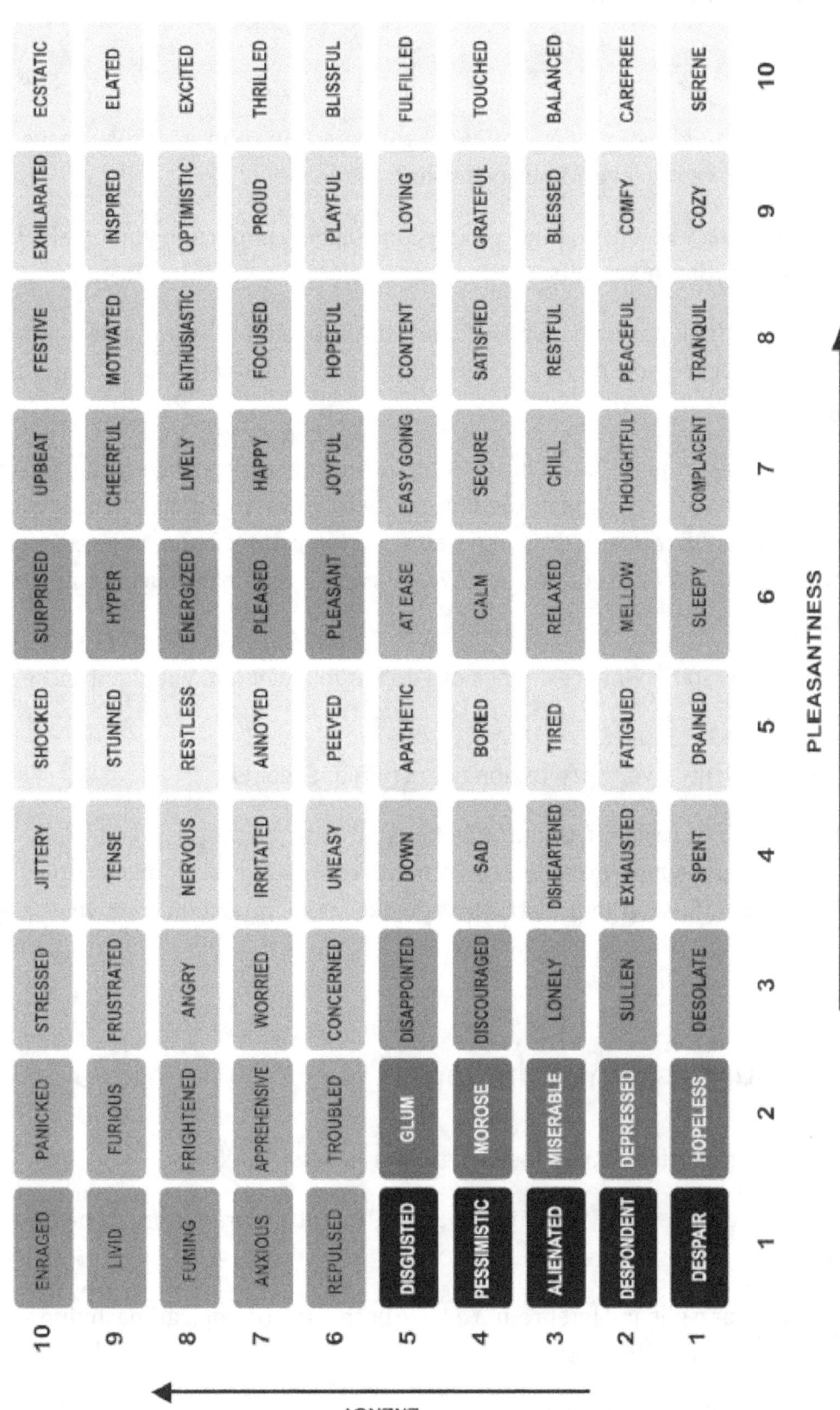

# RESILIENT THINKING

What stood out the most to you as you went through this course? Do you have a stronger awareness of your energy level? Energy drains?

What is the one thing you will do that will have the biggest impact on your goal? Hint: Simple actions can bring profound results.

Keep in mind that high performance and work-life satisfaction is not a destination. It is an ongoing process where you integrate new habits and slowly eliminate habits that do not advance your goals.

Balance may not seem possible at first, so focus on integrating ways you can renew your energy throughout the day. Tune in to your ability to focus and finish, your level of joy and satisfaction, and foundational habits like sleep and hydration. Then, adjust and adapt your routines and your mindset so you can achieve your goals. Support, coaching, and training can make a big difference.

Now that you understand what resilience can do for you, what do you want these skills to do for you?

Take the time to identify your professional and personal goals.

The ultimate value of resilient thinking is being able to accomplish your goals and move forward in your career and life. There is so much competing for your attention today, and the constant pull of these urgent distractions makes it so important to have clearly defined goals.

## Activate Your Resilient Thinking

The following characteristics are consistent with resilient thinking:

1. You anticipate change. Are you thinking about the future or waiting to be told about the next move?

2. You use both your right and left brain. You use both analytic, logical reasoning and creative processing, like your intuition.

3. You are decisive. You can make decisions rather than getting trapped in analysis paralysis.

4. You are open-minded. You do not judge your own suggestions or the suggestions of others; you keep your options open. There is a degree of patience as you consider many options instead of rushing to a decision.

5. You learn from mistakes. You review and revise as you go through your day and learn from the things that do not go so well.

6. You recognize you may have bias and listen to others to learn a new perspective.

High-performance leadership is not something you are born with; it is something you learn. It requires commitment. It's a process where you make intentional and deliberate choices to go beyond complacency and fulfill your potential. This helps you inspire others along the way. When you choose to embrace your potential, you will empower others to do the same.

## Boost Your Resilient Thinking

Ask these questions every week. Keep a journal—online or in a notebook—and write out the answers. Periodically, look back and evaluate yourself. Are you moving in the right direction?

1. What went right?

2. What went wrong?

3. What did I learn from #1 and #2?

4. What is my top priority for next week?

5. What did I waste time on last week?

6. Am I getting in my own way (self-sabotage)?

7. Why am I doing this?

*Complete the Study Questions on the next page.*

**STUDY QUESTIONS**

1. Think of a time when you were stressed at work. How was your body reacting? What were you physically feeling?

2. What is it like when you slow things down and freeze the moment?

3. Have you ever tried journaling? Were you successful or was it a struggle? What can you try differently as you move forward?

Journaling is a great way to enhance mindful attention. As you reflect on the experience and jot down what you notice, you build your situational awareness.

**Additional Thoughts:**

# ACTION PLAN

Check out the module online describing the 100 day roadmap. Using 100 days to achieve goals is an excellent way to monitor and measure your progress.

This module is where you set up your plan to ensure you achieve your goal for this course.

On the next page is a Goal Worksheet to write out your goal.

Use the 100 day map to establish a timeline with due dates and milestones.

# Goal Worksheet

**Goal:**                                                                                    **Date**

I want to


This is important to me RIGHT NOW because




Are you coachable on this issue?       Yes       No

If not, what do you need to do to become coachable?

- ❏ Do you need a mindset shift?
- ❏ Is timing bad because of personal issues?
- ❏ Are you stuck for another reason?

**Notes:**

# NOTES

# BENEFITS OF COACHING

Leaders who engage in coaching take a major step forward. Highly successful people agree that the best advice they ever had was to get a coach. Your sons and daughters have sports coaches, math coaches, there are life coaches and business coaches.

Executives and leaders also need a coach. Not all coaches are created equal, however, and outcomes will depend on how well you define your goals and how focused your goal is to help you achieve that goal. We will equip you to formulate goals that are clear and compelling.

Coaching is a relationship. It is this relationship where you learn to have healthy, open interactions where you can take risks. In our relationship you will be encouraged to be open so you can learn more about you.

**Coaching is powerful in the following situations:**

- Transition
- Rapid growth
- Competitive situations
- New leadership roles
- Changing careers/ roles

Coaching can address one or more of the following:

### Executive Performance

Are there limiting behaviors/ mindsets that interfere with outcomes? We work to shift those toward successful practices that optimize performance in your current role, as well as prepare you for your next one.

### Team Engagement

To advance your agenda, it is important to engage your team. Coaching will help executives craft and communicate a compelling vision, build engagement, ownership, and alignment in their teams.

### Emotional Effectiveness & Agility

Distractions. Demands. Conflict. Navigating change can increase the stress reaction and derail your best efforts. Develop emotional intelligence and resilience. This includes decision making, communication and more.

### Promotion. Branding.

Cultivating personal and professional strengths for a career around your unique skills, passion, and contributions. Developing a strong leadership brand helps you define your value.

## COACHING REALLY WORKS (RESEARCH FINDINGS)

The Personnel Management Association revealed productivity increased to 86% when coaching was added to training. Without coaching, the productivity gain was 22%.

Coaching has a 6:1 return on the investment. Leaders report their relationship with their direct reports and their bosses improved as did:

- Quality
- Productivity
- Outcomes
- Turnover
- Teamwork

The Resilient Leader Coaching program will propel you forward in your current position as well as your career (or business).

Knowing **what you want to achieve** is sometimes the most difficult part of this process. Spend time thinking through what you want and writing it out in a SMART goal.

## Value Contributions (Why Work Smart Coaches are the Best Coach for You):

- Dr. Cynthia Howard has worked with hundreds of leaders and executives and understands the challenges you face. Our approach is based on practical solutions.
- Dr. Howard is a "Coach's Coach," including PhD's, MD's and MSW's to be their best. This expert experience is now yours.
- Our coaches have real world experience as a leader. Dr. Howard has been a manager and Director in large organizations along with entrepreneurial experience managing virtual teams.
- We have personally gone through major transitions, rebranded, and grown.
- Dr. Howard has written 7 books and online programs on leadership, mindset, and performance.
- Pioneer of the Resilient Mindset. Developed the Resilience Pyramid. Certified Scrum Master. Black Belt Lean Six Sigma.

Work Smart Consulting is grounded in the foundations of performance, we understand what is required to get you there.

*Do you know your value contributions? This program will equip you to define and own your superpowers.*

# ABOUT WORK SMART CLUB

The Work Smart Club is an online center for work and well-being. We have a library of tools, strategies, and courses to help you propel your career forward and energize your success.

Technology has changed how we live, work, and communicate, and we recognize it is time to change how we approach work and learning. The online membership has premium resources, course, short 5-to-15-minute training along with on-the-go topics, you can consume quickly, all designed to strengthen your leadership and enhance work life satisfaction.

If you want support, training, and an innovative approach to develop your leadership skills, become a great communicator and consistently achieve your goals, consider joining "the Club."

Worksmartclubnetwork.com

# ABOUT DR. HOWARD

## CYNTHIA HOWARD PhD, LSSBB

Pioneer of the Resilient Mindset.
Executive Coach | Performance Expert.
Fellow, AIS (American Institute of Stress)
Black Belt Lean Sigma
Certified Scrum Master
Licensed Heartmath Trainer & Provider

$20^+$ years of coaching practice, Dr. Howard has worked with leaders, business owners, professionals, helping them move beyond the barriers that limit progress. With a background as a Registered Nurse and graduate degrees in psychology, Cynthia researched what makes individuals successful and what gets in the way of progress.

Working with thousands of people, Cynthia developed the 5 Levels of Resilience Pyramid, organized around mindset, energy management and the science of performance.

**Author:**

3 Seconds to Impact

The Work Smart Principle

365 Power Thoughts for the Resilient Leader

Everyday Emotional Intelligence: A Guide to Better Communication. Learn to Handle Fatal Emotions, Drama, Conflict and Bullying.

105 Tips Work Smart. Think Different.

H.E.A.L: Healthy Emotions. Abundant Life.

# STAY IN TOUCH

*Stay connected to resources, webinars, and free tips on our social media sites.*

Connect with us on Facebook: www.facebook.com/worksmartclub

Connect with us on LinkedIn:

www.linkedin.com/in/drcynthiahoward

www.ingramcontent.com/pod-product-compliance
Lightning Source LLC
Chambersburg PA
CBHW081403290426
44110CB00018B/2476